NEVER SELL AGAIN

(and make more sales than ever before!)

Stan Peake

Advance Praise for Never Sell Again

"Never Sell Again is a must-read for anyone considering a sales role or currently in a sales role. There is an old saying 'People love to buy, but they hate to be sold.' By following the advice Stan provides here you will 'create value' for your buyers by simply helping them make a well-informed buying decision. That's the distinction between predatory sales reps and servant sales reps. It will pay long-term dividends for you in the future."
   - John Hoskins, Author and Founder of Level Five Selling

"'Never Sell Again' is an eye-opening guide that champions the transformation of sales into a service-centric endeavor. The author's insights on becoming a servant leader and forging meaningful connections with clients offer a much-needed shift from the stereotypical pushy salesperson image. This book is a treasure trove of wisdom for individuals looking to grow their sales while remaining authentic, empathetic, and genuinely invested in their clients' success. If you're ready to embark on a journey that transcends traditional sales tactics, "Never Sell Again" is the compass you've been seeking."
   - Catherine Brownlee, President, Alberta Enterprise Group

"Stan Peake captures all the best practices to identify your customer and meet their needs so you can create win-win business relationships. "Never Sell Again" presents the key concepts every business person should know in a quick read book with an effective summary of concepts with examples at the end for easy reference. Having been in leadership roles in both large and multiple small businesses across my career, I have invested a lot in learning business and sales skills. Stan shares the key best practices in a concise, fact-based manner, which I find refreshing and rare."

- Diana Pederson, CEO, DragonFly MedTech

"Never Sell Again is a well-organized book that every CEO and entrepreneur should pass out to all of their colleagues at every level. Great for those who are new and think they are scared to sell a product, a strategy or an idea. It's also a great reminder for well-established and experienced business professionals that will help them keep their saw sharp, organized, and outsmart their competitors. Never Sell Again will help you do the proper due diligence for your potential customer to know more about them and their possible pain points and needs."

- Michael Palmer, Vice President, Operations, Innosol Health

"I always enjoy reading Stan's books to re-center my focus. 'Never Sell Again' is a great read for sales professionals (or anyone) who are feeling stale. Even though you may have attended many sales conferences, trainings, masterclasses or workshops, reading this book is a great way to disconnect from the CRM and social media to refocus on what really attracts clients; meeting their needs first. The funny thing is, this understanding is not just for sales, but it's a way of living your life such that your dreams come to you."

- Dave Barwise, President, DS Security Solutions Inc

"Discovering that selling is truly about serving and helping others was a revelation for me, and "Never sell again' opened my eyes to embrace the power of love and care through sales. A simple shift in mindset and I'm no longer avoiding these conversations."
- Miguel Abasacal, Founder of Thrive Faster and host of the Newcomers ON FIRE! Podcast

"Never Sell Again is an exceptional book that feels like a personal conversation with Stan Peake. It's an enjoyable and enlightening read, filled with valuable knowledge and insights. As you embark on your learning journey with Stan, be sure to have a notepad handy to scribble down the important points and any questions that arise. Rest assured, this book will provide the answers you seek and guide you towards sales success."
- Erik Greenstein, Regional Sales Manager, Parcel Pro and UPS Capital Company

"Never Sell Again is a foundational book for anybody looking to further develop themselves in a client facing role at any level. Along with a step-by-step guide on how to lead with value-based selling, Peake brings us back to the basics of what it means to be a trailblazer in business — lead with curiosity and a willingness to help. The book is well detailed with actionable insight on building meaningful connections, uncovering customer needs, and providing honest solutions. Peake has managed to create an easily digestible guide that will help you form a new and positive perspective on selling. I highly recommend buying this book!"
-    Layla Binesh, Sales Leader, New York/ Amsterdam

Never Sell Again
(and make more sales than ever before!)

Let me guess.
You're reading this book because the title grabbed you.
You might be a consultant, therapist, coach, chiropractor, fitness trainer, or any other profession that helps people.
You got into this business to help others, not to sell.
Am I getting warm?
If so, this book is for you.
This book is for any professional who needs to grow their business or career, but who doesn't want to become a snake oil salesperson, or sell their soul to do so.
This book does not contain a slick or fancy system. Zero mention of overcoming objections or manipulating people.
This book is designed to help you help more people, and in doing so, help your own bottom line.
If this sounds like the book you were hoping for, grab a pen or highlighter, and let's get to it.
This book will be right up your alley, but you've still got work to do. This book might change your career trajectory, but there are no miracle cures to be found, just solid fundamentals you can choose to apply to be more successful, or not. My hope is that you will embrace the tools and philosophies that you are about to read.
They have helped a lot of other professionals see more success, and help more of the people they are aiming to help.

To your success,

Table of Contents

Never Sell Again

Picture this:

You're behind on rent.
Bills are piling up.
You don't know where your next paycheck is coming from.

You have a window of hope in the form of a sales meeting at 3:00 p.m.
You really, really need this commission. It's a big one, too.

How do you show up?

Are you calm, confident and poised for success? Or are you sweating, with your heart racing, feeling anxious or nervous, and looking like a door-to-door encyclopedia salesperson who's about to go broke? Which of these emotional states do you think would be more likely to lead to a sale?

As an executive coach, I'm often reminding my clients that our focus dictates our state, and our state influences the state of our prospective buyer. What does that mean? Well let's consider the famous studies cited by Dr Mehrabian on communication in his book "Silent Messages". Dr Mehrabian and his team found that selling to prospects had a lot to do with communication. They reported that communication can be broken down as 55% body language, 38% paralanguage and 7% the actual words we use[1]. This means that 93% of all communication is nonverbal[1]. Hold that thought.

You've probably also heard that we only use 10% of our brains. This is simply not true. What is true is that approximately 10% of our decisions are made consciously. In other words, 90% of our decisions are made subconsciously.

Think about it. Are you deciding to breathe right now, or is that happening subconsciously? Are you thinking about what muscles to contract so that you don't slump over, or is that being done for you subconsciously? Even when you drive to work or school, if you're repeating the same route that you do every day, your entire drive can happen subconsciously. Have you ever arrived at your destination only to realize you seem like you just woke up, and the entire drive your mind was elsewhere? This is the power of our subconscious mind, and how many decisions are made without us having to think.

Bringing us back: how does this all relate to sales?
Well, if 93% of all communication is nonverbal[1] and 90% of our decisions are made without us thinking about it, then the overwhelming majority of how we make an impression on someone is happening without us actually thinking about it. Think about yawning. Chances are when someone beside you yawns, you do too. That's how easily we are influenced by other people. It's also how easily we influence others. Let's go back to that feeling of desperately needing your next sale.

Think about your body language.
Are you calm, welcoming, comforting and appealing to be around? Or are you tense, rigid and visibly nervous? Remember that 55% of all communication is body language[1]. Do you consciously decide what posture to assume? Most of us don't. For most people, our emotions manifest through our body language. We feel angry, and

then we tense our bodies. We feel joy, and then we smile. We basically advertise how we are feeling. So how does this all relate back to sales? It all comes down to three simple words.

Know, Like, Trust

There's an old saying in sales that before anyone buys anything from you, they need to know you, like you and trust you. If we want a complete stranger to know us, like us and trust us, doesn't it make sense that we need to appear approachable, likeable and trustworthy? How does our nervous, anxious, tense state help us achieve that? As you probably guessed, it doesn't.

Dan Pink, in his book 'To Sell is Human' conducted a massive study called 'what do you really do at work[2]?' Pink and his team found that although only nine to ten percent of the North American population works in sales, 40% of our time, regardless of job title, is spent in what he calls 'non-sales selling[2]'. In other words, 40% of our time is spent in sales-like behaviors[2]. Dan Pink cites negotiating for budget dollars, exchanging resources or competing for the boardroom or meeting space as examples of non-sales selling[2]. Although only nine to ten percent of the North American population work in sales, we all need to understand how to better persuade, negotiate or bargain, because it's how we spend 40% of our working days[2].

For any entrepreneurs, salespeople or business leaders, especially consultants, coaches or those working in the information economy, it is essential to build trust in our target audience. In most cases, people aren't buying our product or service - they are buying *us*. In keeping with the know, like, trust philosophy, we must build an environment of trust. What does an environment of trust look like for our buyer?

Trust looks relaxed, calm and patient. We can detect trust when we notice open body postures, engaged facial features, and when our prospect is asking questions. We feel trust when we feel warmth, laughter, engagement and curiosity.

We notice an absence of trust with arms crossed or closed body positions. Perhaps your prospect is looking at their watch, or even rolling their eyes. A prospect who does not trust will be hasty with their words, limited with their questions, and possibly even interrupt you in the middle of asking your questions.

A prospect who trusts is in the process of a decision. they may or may not buy, but they are considering it. A prospect who does not trust has already made a decision. They are about to leave your office, or they are just being polite enough until they feel it's okay to do so.

Remember that our state influences the state of others. Our state influences our buyers' state. If we are anxious, rushed, tense and desperate for a sale, our state will be obvious. Our buyer wants to know us, like us and trust us. If they perceive that we are anxious, stressed, nervous or desperate, they will not trust us. They will detect that something is off, even if they don't know what it is. Whatever they feel that is off will be enough to get in the way of building trust, and making a purchase.

No trust = no sale

Keep in mind that it is not our prospect's job to be our coach and put us in the ideal state to build rapport and make a sale. That's our job.

It is not our prospect's job to self-regulate their emotions and be as open as possible and receptive to a sale. That's our job.

You do not have to be an expert coach to put your prospect at ease. You just need to coach yourself. So how do you that?

Remember that our focus dictates our state. If we are focused on making the sale, our state is about a transaction. We tend to make this transaction or event bigger than it is. We become nervous about this impending event. We get far too focused on an outcome, rather than remaining present. It starts to feel like a 'make or break' scenario.

If we change our focus however, we can change our state. Let's think about what state we must be in to put our prospect in their ideal state. What state do we want our prospect in? Calm, relaxed, open, present and engaged.

The best way to help our prospects become calm, relaxed, open, present and engaged is for us to not only model these emotions, but to actually feel them. If our focus dictates our state and our goal state is calm, relaxed, open, present and engaged, then what can we focus on to help us get there?

Focusing on the sale will not get us there. Focusing on targets will not get us there. There is only one way to arrive at our desired state. We must choose our focus and that focus must be on helping our customer to the best of our abilities.

Think about how you felt the last time you helped someone. Maybe it was your child that skinned their knee, or an elderly person across the street, or maybe you helped direct traffic until the police arrived after witnessing a minor accident. Do you remember how you felt? Did you feel anxious, nervous, stressed and tense, or did you have that warm feeling inside and you felt good about yourself; even good about who you are? Helping others is one of the most profound feelings we can experience. It is when we are at our very best!

When you go on a date, do you roll out of bed, put dirty clothes on, and show up at the restaurant? Or do you shower, brush your teeth, pick out your best clothes and even give yourself a pep talk to show up as the best version of yourself? Of course, it's the latter - but why? It's because we are trying to create the best impression possible with the person we are trying to date.

Why would sales be any different? By showing up in a stressed state, we may as well be showing up disheveled with the wrong uniform on, not knowing our product or service, or how it compares to our prospects' other alternatives.

Far more important than knowing product specs or even your value proposition, is to show up as the best version of yourself. The best version of yourself is that version that is focused on helping others.

Focusing on helping others has other benefits too. In addition to putting us in the ideal emotional and physical state, it also helps us become a better professional.

Helping helps us get better

In his book 'Level 5 Selling', John Hoskins breaks down different types of sales people. I've given clients this book almost as much as I've handed out our previous bestseller 'How to Sell in Any Economy'. Hoskin's describes the five different approaches to selling from level one to level five. Without giving away any spoilers, we are going to focus on the level four salesperson.

A level four salesperson acts in a way like a coach by doing two things. These two things are the two most important skills for any salesperson in this author's opinion. Those two quintessential skills are;
1. Asking great questions, and
2. Listening with your whole body.

Asking questions, listening to your prospect, and then positioning your product or service as an answer to their challenges or goals is also called inquiry- or discovery-based selling.

Basically, we are asking questions to discover your prospects' pain points, problems, goals and needs, and then positioning your product or service as their ultimate solution. In other words, your value proposition is the answer to a question that has been plaguing your prospect.

Level four salespeople outperform level one, two or three by orders of magnitude by selling this way[3]. Simply put, they make way more sales because they are better at helping their customers solve their problems and achieve their goals.

(Since I know your curiosity is getting the better of you, level 5 sales people act as strategic partners for their prospects[3]. They actually become like a business partner of sorts. To find out more, read Level Five Selling).

Another benefit of focusing on helping our customer is less memorization. Think about it this way. You can either spend countless hours honing and perfecting an elevator pitch that you think will work 100 times out of 100, or you can come up with a perfect pitch every time based on what your customer has just told you.

Consider it this way. You ate today, didn't you? So did almost everyone else on the planet. Did you all eat for the same reason? Of course not. Some people treat food as fuel. They eat to fuel their bodies and perform at the highest of their abilities. Other people eat for enjoyment; they love that slice of chocolate cake or glass of fine wine. Others eat because they are famished. Perhaps they worked through lunch or they have financial struggles. In short, if we don't eat, we die, and yet our reasons for eating can be vastly different from one person to another.

If our reasons for eating (which we need to do for survival) can be different from person to person, clearly our reasons for buying can be vastly different from person to person. This means it's nearly impossible to come up with the perfect pitch that could work for everyone. Instead of a one size fits all solution, great salespeople need to find *one size fits one* solutions. That's exactly what happens if we can be present, ask great questions and then listen with our whole body.

Your prospect will tell you everything you need to know to nail your pitch every time. This is because it's not a pitch. They will likely tell you what they do, and who they do it for. They might even divulge the challenges they are facing in their business (aka their pain points).

By listening to them and then recommending your business, because of how it solves their problems, you are not making a sale; you are providing a valuable service. You are not just a salesperson. You are a valuable member of the service team.

Always remember that your prospect is there for a reason. People don't like to waste their own time. Blockbuster failed because people would rather push a button on a remote in their home while wearing their pajamas than go to the store and see what physical inventory is there, wait in the line and make sure to come back within two to three days, or else be charged a late fee. I'm old enough to remember being charged for not rewinding the VHS tape as well.

The fact that people don't like to waste their own time means that your prospect is there acting in their own best interests. They want to be there. In fact, they might *need* to be there.

If you've created your ideal customer profile (ICP), also known as your ideal client avatar, then you already know the demographics and psychographics behind your ideal customer. You know who they are, you know where they are, and you know how they think. If you know that, then you know your customer is there because they have pain points they're trying to solve. They have problems they need a solution for. They have needs. They have goals they would like to achieve.

Your job is not to sell your prospect anything. Your job is to solve the problems and pain points for your customer, and help them achieve their goals. What feels better; selling something, or helping someone?

You may have heard that nice guys finish last. You might think that you need to break the rules, or have a taste for blood to succeed in sales. I disagree. That being said, good guys still have to show up and do the work. Keep in mind that your prospect has needs. They came to you, or are willing to take a meeting with you, in order to find a solution to those needs and problems.

You also know that competition is fierce. There are thousands, maybe even millions of others out there that are trying to do what you do. Many others will view your prospect as a walking commission, not a person. There are thousands, if not millions of people that are willing to take your customers money, and not care whether or not they actually help them. This means it is in your customer's best interest for them to do business with you, if you actually care about them. This also means that your job is not to sell. In fact, this isn't even about your job. If your customers came to you with a problem, and you can help them, then it is your moral obligation to do so.

It is your moral duty to help your customer to the best of your ability so that they do not get scammed by someone else who takes their money and fails to follow through.

Throughout my career, I have coached several other coaches, from health coaches to executive coaches, business coaches, fitness coaches and more. It's been my experience through hundreds of examples that those who get into industries to help people seem to have a disconnect between providing the service and charging money for it.

I have worked with people who have literally saved lives, who clam up when it comes to talking about what they do or describing their services to a prospect. It's as though they feel selling the service takes all of the Integrity out of it. Most service providers (and I include doctors, nurses and therapists here too) would much rather help people all day long, and let someone else do all of the sales.

Unfortunately, this doesn't work if it's your own business, or if you don't want to leave your livelihood up to somebody else. What has helped many of these professionals better position their service is removing the words 'sales' or 'selling' from their vocabulary entirely. Instead, we use terms like *service* or even *pre-contract service* and *post-contract service* (the work you do before the sale, and the work you do after the sale).

In effect, the service delivery we provide for a potential customer starts when they Google us, pick up the phone or walk in our doors, and it does not stop until we've completely solved their problem (or several problems). Philosophically, it's a continuous act of helping our target market.

The signing of a service agreement or purchase order is merely a transactional step in the end-to-end service delivery. This is the entire philosophy of Never Sell Again. A sale is merely a transaction. We're not really after that, are we? For most of us, what we're really after is a long-term relationship with multiple opportunities to serve our customer, and have them refer us more friends like themselves that we can help. It's about winning the long game.

It's not about closing a deal or manipulating them, or getting their 'share of wallet'. It's about helping people to the best of our abilities, and when we do that, we get more opportunities to help others. Put another way, the more people we help, the more sales we end up making. We go from a single soldier having to do all of the work, to leading a sales team made up of our customers, most of whom don't even want a paycheck!

One more way that focusing on helping our customer helps us become better salespeople is in the numbers. You've heard the expression that sales is a numbers game. If we are focused on making our number, then cold calling, sending emails or LinkedIn reach outs, or direct messaging people on other social media platforms can feel like work. It can feel soulless and it can feel meaningless and never ending.

Look at the numbers from a sales standpoint. A great salesperson might do 100 reach outs a day. Some entrepreneurs I've coached tell me that before working together they would do less than five reach outs a week, some even less than five *per month*!

Making 100 reach outs everyday would place a sales professional in rockstar status based on their volume of outbound sales attempts. Even so, cold calling typically has less than a 10% conversion ratio. This might not even mean closed sales, but booked meetings through the number of people you reached out to. Let's say for every hundred people you reach out to, you end up booking 10 meetings. Chances are, it's less than five these days.

Of those five to ten meetings, seeing as some were cold calls or cold LinkedIn or email reach outs, chances are two or three don't even show up. Of the two to eight meetings we do end up having, a good salesperson might close half. This means one to four sales from 100 reach outs. One to four percent success rate - if they're good! Those sales numbers are enough to take the wind out of anyone's proverbial sails.

Let's look at those numbers from a different perspective. If you are focused on helping others, every sale is a person that you've helped from start to finish. Instead of thinking about closing percentages or conversion rates, we can focus on opportunities to help others. Instead of a lost commission, it's a lost opportunity to help someone.

Statistics show that on average, a sale can take five to 12 points of contact[4]. Most salespeople do not have the bandwidth, the resilience, the motivation or even the desire to reach out to every prospect five to 12 times.

If we shift our focus to helping and caring about our customers, we might not ever give up. We might reach out 30 times asking a prospect if they're ready for us to solve their problem, provide a solution or help them achieve their goal. Philosophically, when should you give up? The answer might be never. Think of how many people you would help if you never gave up on anyone. Think of how many sales that would be, and what that would do for your business, your career, or your life!

Never Sell Again works online

The concept of Never Selling Again also applies online. While some business owners and professionals are naturally gifted content creators on social media, many others struggle, or even detest posting on LinkedIn, Facebook or Twitter. If we embrace the Never Sell Again philosophy, it helps us engage and help our audience online as well.

Just like body language and paralanguage heavily influence communication in person; content, context and subtext influence how we communicate online. No one can see our body language or hear our tone when we post, but that doesn't mean that we are only communicating with the words we type. Our online audience gets to know our subtext (for better or worse) over time.

When we post online, we are entering what's called 'the sea of noise'. Every day, the average North American will see more than 10,000 marketing impressions[5]. Remember how 90% of our decisions are subconscious? One thing that keeps our subconscious mind busy all day is suppressing those images so that we can stay present in a conversation, not get hit by a vehicle crossing the street or not hit someone else when we're driving our vehicle.

Our mind actively blocks out most of these 10,000 images, impressions, logos and ads so that we can function in our busy lives. That's good news for us getting through a day without being overwhelmed, but it's bad news for anyone who's trying to connect with their ideal customer through marketing means. This means every time we post on social media, we have to find ways to be relevant, meaningful, memorable, and ideally incite action in our desired audience. It's very hard to do that by being salesy with our posts.

Of course, you want to sell your products, or book customers in to discovery calls for your service. That's *your need*. What is *your customers' need*? The truth is, sometimes even your customer doesn't know. This is why when we post online or send a newsletter, we can't be selling all of the time. By focusing on helping when we post, we have the opportunity to educate, entertain and engage. Sometimes we even teach our potential customers about problems they didn't even know they had. Other times we help them feel at ease that they're not alone, or we give a name and hope for a solution to a problem they have been experiencing. Sometimes, our customer even teaches us, through polls, or commenting on posts that are designed to drive engagement, not just sales.

Thought leaders who focus on helping, educating, engaging and entertaining often end up building a loyal audience who feels almost like they owe them something. When those thought leaders eventually do post about their new book, new course or new signature program, a decent subset of their audience feels indebted to them. For many of these loyal followers, if they're considering a purchase at all, there's no decision - they go straight to the person who's helped them so much for free all of this time.

Social media posts that are clearly and obviously trying to sell something rarely engage, unless it's a celebrity coming out with their new clothing or make-up line. In fact, even many of the most successful launches by celebrities are not sell-first.

When Dwayne "the Rock" Johnson co-founded his tequila brand Teremana, it was one of the most successful spirit launches of all time; over one million cases sold less than three years after inception[6]. With 388 million followers on Instagram, Johnson is one of the most popular celebrities on the planet.

Johnson's first Instagram post about Teremana was September 26th, 2019, several months before its launch. The post was a picture of the founding team, and the text described the journey of years of crafting their spirit, and thanking his fans for their patience. There was no link to buy, nor mention of where to buy it. Johnson simply stated he thought people would like it, and included the hashtag #ComeHaveaDrinkWithMe

In most cases, for the average-sized audience, for the average entrepreneur or professional, posts designed to sell flop. However, even if your online audience is relatively small, anyone has the chance to go viral with content that truly engages. Posts that ask a question or lead to great discussion or contemplation can often reach a critical mass where it seemingly goes worldwide.

In 2021 I Wrote a post to promote the book "Life Literacy" that I co-authored with Matt Young and Nelson Soh. That post got around 250 views. Earlier that year I wrote a post highlighting several of the major adversities I faced in my life, but how each one was worth it because it led to the book signing for that same book Life Literacy. That post got nearly 115,000 views. Why? because I wasn't trying to sell with that post; I was telling a story, and I was being authentic – letting people get to know me, not just what I was selling.

Not everyone has survived a heart attack or broken their back, or been bullied or gone through all the challenges of owning or co-owning eight businesses that I described in that viral post. On the other hand, everybody has faced adversity, and facing adversity is a universally relatable topic.

Back in 2017 I filmed a video for social media that was targeted specifically at entrepreneurs. This post was designed to reassure, not to sell. I even spoke the words "I'm not trying to sell anything". In this video, I went on to say that just because you're struggling while running your business does not mean that you're a failure as an entrepreneur. I talked about the hardships, the daily realities and the not-so-daily challenges that entrepreneurs face.

My entire goal with this post was to normalize the challenges that entrepreneurs face, instead of glorifying the rare moments of sheer bliss or utter success. Most of us are not partying on a yacht or 'making it rain' in the club!

I wanted entrepreneurs to feel that they weren't alone. I wanted to create psychological safety, and a sense of community for all those founders working so hard, often in isolation. The irony is that I had a prospect reach out to me after seeing that video. They told me that this was probably the seventh or eighth post of mine that they had seen, and that it was the post that convinced them that I was the right coach for them. This client hired me and we worked together for three years.

I could have spent $5,000 or more promoting a different post trying to sell something, and it probably wouldn't have brought in as much revenue as a post where I was not trying to sell anything!

You never have to sell again, but you do have to work

Before I make it seem too easy to Never Sell Again and still make more sales than ever before, I want to be clear that to do so requires four things.

First, this is not some sales system that can be hacked. You can't fake caring. You can't fake being there. You can't fake wanting to help your target customer. The great news about that is that this is not the kind of system that the slimy snake oil salesperson that we all dread can use. This system only works for the good guys.

Secondly, this system does require hard work. It requires hard work, but maybe not in the way that you think. You might be thinking this requires hard work to go out and find all kinds of people to potentially help. To a degree that's true, but the real work happens when someone tells you what they are looking for.

The work begins at this point, not because your clients' problems are hard to solve, but because if you truly care about your customer, you cannot walk away while their problems remain unresolved. In fact, ending every customer interaction with the question "is there anything else I can help you with?" is a staple among hospitality businesses' service training for a simple, yet profound reason. You can't ask 'what else can I help you with?' if you haven't solved the customers' first issue.

Like these successful hospitality businesses, being able to Never Sell Again and still make more sales is contingent on you solving their problem(s). It requires you to follow through; being relentless in the pursuit of customer satisfaction. It's going the extra mile, and it's not stopping until you reach the finish line.

The third aspect of work with the Never Sell Again philosophy is that you do need to help your customer cross the finish line. You may or may not ask for the sale, but your customer does need to make a purchase in order to receive the benefit of your product or service. In this sense, you might be an encourager, a challenger, a supporter, or even a cheerleader.

Think of what you would do to support a friend who is trying to start a new health habit, or quit an unhealthy habit like smoking. You'd be there for them, asking how their process is going, and what they need from you. This is akin to the service you provide for your customer while they are making a purchase decision. A values-based salesperson would not harass their customer to get them to sign a contact. What you can do, and should do, is follow up, encourage, ask clarifying questions, and help your customer commit to and start the process required to reap the benefit your product or service provides.

Remember – it's your moral obligation to help your customer to the fullest of your abilities. They don't get help if they don't buy the software that can save them time and money, or go to the gym to meet with their trainer. Help them cross the finish line and start seeing the benefits you provide.

The fourth element of 'work' involved with the Never Sell Again philosophy is that you should leave your house once in a while. Yes, you have to go out in public, even though virtual platforms have made working from home so seamless. It's important to get out there and network to meet more people, and get to, and stay, top-of-mind for your network when it comes to your profession.

As an extrovert, it's not lost on me that networking and meeting people can feel like work, especially for my more introverted colleagues. While there is no one size fits all solution, it is important for any business professional, especially entrepreneurs and sales professionals, to get out there and network. The old cliché is true: your network is your net worth. Remember what comes before a prospect liking you and trusting you enough to buy from you? They have to get to know you in the first place.

While platforms like Zoom help us to 'shrink the world' and meet virtually with people all over the world, there is no replacement for the real connection that occurs face to face. According to a 2009 study by Forbes, 84% of professionals prefer to meet in person, and 85% feel that in-person meetings lead to better connections[7].

Perhaps it doesn't have to be an intimidating networking event with dozens (or hundreds) of strangers. Author Julie Hiner has attended a lot of book launches for other authors, and as an author herself, she always buys a copy to support the author. To Julie, it helps reinforce a very supportive local community of authors, who end up reciprocating by attending her launch parties and purchasing her books. This also leads Julie to have a stockpile of books, most of which she's able to offer as door prizes or giveaways at her launch parties. This saves money, and adds incentive for more people to come to each book launch.

Julie has also partnered with a local rock band who plays at all of her book launches. Not only does this double her audience by way of the bands' followers, but she grows her readership and fanbase every show through a subset of the band's fans. Conversely, the band wins by growing their fanbase each show through Julie's readers who get to see the band for the first time. Win-win thinking is at the heart of the Never Sell Again methodology

In order to Never Sell Again, you must be organized. Unless you have a photographic memory, you need a system. Nothing says "I don't care" like forgetting a customer or prospect's name, or important details about their business or their life. A consummate professional knows this, and makes a concerted effort to demonstrate their care. It could be sending a birthday card, or even a birthday email. Perhaps it's customized gifts.

In his book "The Richest Real Estate Agent", Ben Oosterveld shares the story of a real estate agent who gifted one of their clients two bottles of fine wine after learning that this was a passion of theirs[8]. For another client he did not get to know well due to a speedy listing and purchase cycle, he made a game out of the realtor's gift by giving his clients five envelopes marked as different days of the week[8]. In each envelope was a gift card. Neither of these gifts cost much, but the impact, according to Oosterveld, was profound.

Gift-giving can be a system as demonstrated through these examples. It's also important to have a system for remembering your prospects company, position, email and other details. Unless you have that photographic memory, this is where your customer relationship management

(CRM) software can come in handy. Many sales professionals use their CRM simply for customer acquisition and monitoring the sales process. True service professionals can use their CRM as a customer satisfaction tool as well.

Having a system for email or phone follow-ups is also essential. Sales professionals talk about warm versus cold leads. Nothing makes a warm lead cool off faster than forgetting about them. Often, it's less about how you follow up, and more about when you follow up. It must be authentic; although it also needs to be organized if you're dealing with multiple prospects at any given time. We're human. We forget stuff.

I've even seen pre-revenue start-ups forget to follow up with potential paying customers. You think that would be their only priority, but when you have several leads on the go, it can be easier than you think to forget about Tom who you met at that chamber of commerce event three weeks ago.

Using a CRM like HubSpot, Zoho, or SalesForce can help organize proven behaviors that increase conversion and buying rates. By using your CRM or even Microsoft Excel or your written day timer intentionally, you can build the right helpful behaviors.

My business partner Matt Young is very intentional about mixing his modalities when it comes to follow up. He might send an email, then tag his network on Twitter, then send an article or documentary or a book to a potential prospect as a means of helping them at every step of the sales cycle. While he changes up what he sends, he does so with intentionality, even scheduling these activities. This attention and intention with the details have helped him win customers that in some cases, took up to five years to land!

I even use this process as an author. My next book is about leadership. I've conducted a lot of research on leadership development, and I've also interviewed the top leaders I could get in front of. I organized my interview prospecting efforts in a Microsoft Word document. I wrote down everybody I hoped to interview, and then my first attempt and date, second, third, fourth, all the way up to seventh.

While many of the leaders that I reached out to didn't require seven follow-ups, I wanted to organize my system based on not giving up. The more successful the people you are trying to reach become, the more people vying for their attention, and the busier they get. I call the approach I take with this level of follow up *approachable relentlessness*. Never give up, but never bother anyone or come across as pushy.

Many startup founders find themselves in the position of needing to raise capital. Raising capital for many can be even more difficult than the process of selling. The Never Sell Again philosophy applies here too. Just as your customer has needs that we should focus on, so do investors. As a startup founder, your pitch deck is where most founders think to stand out from other ventures seeking investment. Rather than struggling with finding ways to stand out through your pitch deck, shift your focus.

Your investor has pain points too. According to research, 30% of all venture capital backed startups fail[9]. This means 30% of the companies the investor you are talking to has invested in fail. As a result, your would-be investor might be risk-averse. They might start to develop a little bit of a 'gun-shy' mentality. The more you learn about your investor, the more you can uncover about their background, their career, their passions and their interests.

You might be trying to gain capital for your growing business, but what you're really doing is selling (negotiating, bartering, exchanging aka non-sales selling) with another human being[2]. Perhaps you know other investors who aren't looking to invest in your start-up, but might want to contribute to the venture capital fund of the investor you are meeting with. Just like a potential customer, the more you learn about a potential investor's pain points, problems, goals and needs, the more likely you are to secure funding.

Last but not least, the Never Sell Again philosophy requires self-awareness. By self-awareness, I mean both personal and organizational. It often requires both. What I mean by self-awareness is an awareness of your strengths, weaknesses and value proposition as an entrepreneur, service provider, or on behalf of your company (or product or service).

While you don't want to be a walking encyclopedia (this is a level three sales person according to John Hoskins[3]), you do have to know how your product or service stacks up against your competition.

Most importantly, you must intimately understand your value proposition. In most cases, your value proposition is multifaceted or layered, and differs from person to person, even when selling the same product or service.

This is because value is in the eye of the beholder.

What is your value proposition?

In 2019 I was giving a keynote speech for a conference in Calgary, Alberta titled "what is your value proposition?" As fate would have it, that morning I was doing my last speech rehearsal at a cooperative workspace in downtown Calgary. There was a long hallway, which was full of paintings, all by local artists. One of the paintings, which was probably four feet wide and four feet tall, was completely covered in black paint. That was it.

At that time, my son Chase was 10 years old. He could have created that painting by the looks of it. That painting was for sale for $2,500, by the way. Spoiler alert: I didn't buy it. Maybe someone else would be moved immeasurably by that painting because to them it represented angst or joy or pain. Who knows? I saw it as only worth the canvas - maybe less because it was covered in black paint, and nothing else. I was not the target customer. For me, this held no value. For someone else, this held at least $2,500 in value. Value is in the eye of the beholder. I shared that story in my speech that day, and it helped the audience understand value proposition and customer focus in a whole new way.

As an executive coach, I work with driven entrepreneurs trying to grow their business, and driven executives and leaders who want to become more worth following. Because they have different goals, they are usually looking for different things when it comes to the value they'd assign to a coach. When I meet with potential clients who are entrepreneurs, I focus my background (when it comes up) on my lived experience in entrepreneurship. I talk about the Entrepreneurship and Innovation program I completed at Harvard Business School Online. I mention the sales leadership program I completed at Queens University. We discuss how my business partner and I sold our business in 2009. I probably give them a copy of my previous bestsellers I've written on sales and entrepreneurship. I also talk about the many clients I've helped start, grow or even sell their companies.

When I'm speaking with a potential executive client, I focus my value proposition on the graduate education I completed in values-based leadership at Royal Roads University. I discuss the 20+ years I have of lived experience in leadership positions, and being part of the executive team in five different companies. I talk about the different boards of directors I've served on. I discuss my role as a corporate facilitator, and how my team and I have facilitated team-builders or strategic planning sessions for nearly a decade. Lastly, I talk about the hundreds of leaders I've worked with whom I've helped get promoted or land the job of their dreams, and develop the potential of their teams.

I'm not being a chameleon by telling two different stories. I simply adjust the experiences and credentials I disclose, based on how it can help the prospective client in front of me. Chances are, your product or service is no different. You might sell the same model of car to eight different people, who all bought for different reasons. One might have loved the power or pick-up speed, while another customer loved that they could fit their whole family and their camping gear. Yet another customer may have purchased because of the fuel economy, or even the color.

Even if you don't have different customer segments like I do, or sell products with various features, chances are your value proposition will differ from one potential prospect to the next. How would you know what features or benefits of your product or service to focus on? By asking great questions and listening with your whole body. You would know if you are focused on helping your customer, not focused on making a sale.

When you ask questions about your prospects' life or business (depending on your focus), you will find out their pain points, their problems, their goals and their needs. When you know this, you understand what they need if you have that self-awareness as a professional, and experience in your field. With this experience and with self-awareness, your value proposition simply becomes recommendation-based selling.

For the first 18 years of my professional career I worked in fitness, health and medical. I often use the following analogy when it comes to explaining recommendation-based selling.

If a client came to me at that time who wanted to lose 30 pounds, rehabilitate a knee injury and run their first marathon, then I wasn't trying to sell them package A or package B from a sales presentation binder.

I would recommend working with a fitness trainer several times a week, as well as a dietitian or nutritionist to help them achieve their weight loss goal, and gain the necessary strength, endurance, flexibility and fitness to achieve their goal of running a marathon. That trainer would prescribe a running program with progressive mileage to help them achieve their goal without risking an overuse injury. I would also recommend at the onset of their program, that this client see, and potentially work with, a physiotherapist who could diagnose and help rehabilitate their knee injury.

If this client was seeing challenges along the way with commitment to their program, I would recommend that they also see a life coach or health coach.

The above set of recommendations are not an 'off-the-shelf' program. I wasn't selling them 'package B'; I just asked them what they were here for. I got to know them, I got to understand what they wanted and needed, and then built custom solutions.

I understand it's different if you're selling cars. It doesn't really matter what you're selling however; we can all still customize our solutions, or what product or service we recommend based on the pain points, problems and needs and goals that our questions uncover when we focus on helping our customer. Given the car example on page 42, you might sell the exact same product eight times in a row, yet focus on different features and benefits of that product every single time.

Ask questions, listen, and then respond with what they need. If what they need isn't your product or service, be honest. They will thank you, and often even refer you business, after they don't buy from you.

Remember that you are not selling, you are providing a service. If your product is not what they need, the service they need is for you to tell them just that.

Finally, when it comes to crafting your value proposition, there is a formula and a process. The simple formula can be crafted as either:

"I/we help X to achieve Y" or

"I/we help X to Y".

In this equation, X = your target audience or ideal customer profile (ICP), and Y = the goals you help them achieve or problems you help them solve.

As a process, there are three key steps. Adapted from an article I originally wrote for Business 2 Community[10], this process follows below:

Step One: Identify your Ideal Customer Avatar

If your business is in the direct business to consumer (B2C) space, you are reverse-engineering a person. If you're a business to business (B2B) provider, you are coming up with the ideal business you'd love to serve. The parameters change, though the process is identical.

Using one trait per Post-It® note (I should own stock in 3M by now!), list off all of the demographic information you know about your ideal customer. Hypothesize about what you don't know. Examples would be as follows;

Demographics

Business to Consumer (B2C) example

Location	Residential community, neighborhood, City, or State/ Province. Hone in to the level of detail most beneficial to your marketing or sales strategy
Income	Household income (example $150,000)
Occupation	Dentist
Age	35 – 65 years of age
Family info	Married with three children

Business to Business (B2B) example

Annual revenue	$2M – $5M
Industry	Industry, including any niche (example railway construction)
Business stage	Start up, scale up, etc
Target customer	Often the more you know about who the company you want to sell to is focused on selling to, the more you can help them, because you can enhance their value proposition

Once you've brainstormed (or listed, if you have the available data) the key demographic typifiers of your ideal customer, it's time to repeat the exercise for their psychographics. More important than where they live and work – is how they think; how, when and why they make their purchase decisions.

Important psychographic considerations for an individual might include their goals, their values, their career objectives, and even their relationship with their family, coworkers, boss or neighbors. Think about renting or buying a house. If you were in your second year of college, you'd most likely want to live near other young people. They'd be less likely to file noise complaints every weekend. On the other hand, if you had a young family and busy career, you'd most likely be asking the realtor about the family situation (read: lifestyle) of your neighbors. They even made a movie called Bad Neighbors based on this premise.

Psychographic considerations for a business might include when they need to submit a budget, whether or not a potential vendor aligns with their organizational values, and who they are competing against (and how that drives their competitive spirit and strategy). Of course, who they sell to, and what they sell, would be key considerations as you consider how and why your product or service adds value to the companies you try and sell to.

A very popular meme circulating social media in 2023 demonstrates the difference between demographics and psychographics. The meme depicts two men;
- Both born in 1948
- Both raised in the UK
- Both have been married twice
- Both live in a castle
- Both are wealthy and famous.

Based on all of the above information, a marketing team would be tempted to develop a strategy to find more individuals like this, speaking to their reality. That being said, when you find out who these individuals are, would you really try to sell to King Charles III the same way you'd approach Ozzy Osbourne? Probably not.

Getting back to crafting your three-step value proposition, you will know that your work is complete through this first step when you have a crystal-clear picture of the individual you are looking to sell to, or you can imagine yourself walking the halls (or through the warehouse as the case may be) of the business you're trying to supply to or service. When you can visualize the meeting, and what questions you might ask, or even what questions your prospect might ask, you've done your due diligence.

Step Two: Understand their pain, goals, and needs

Once you have that clear picture in mind, the next Post-it® exercise is to brainstorm all of the perceived (or known) pain points that your ideal customer faces. Start with their pain points, remembering that most people aim to avoid pain more than they seek out pleasure when it comes to their purchase decisions[4].

Keep in mind that your customers' pain is not just associated with your product or service. They also may be kept up at night by competition, dwindling profits (or losing money), imposter syndrome, leading a team, or their children's hectic school and sports schedule. Focus on the likely pain points your ideal customer would be facing, tied to their position, industry, and any other information you know about them.

With their pain points listed, shift your focus to their goals, both personally and professionally; as well as individually and organizationally. As the old sales cliché goes, we tend to reach for painkillers before we take our vitamins.

Finally, narrow the focus on your scope of services, and what your ideal customer needs you for. What does success in your transaction or working relationship look like to them? If you don't know, this is where customer interviews or focus groups can be particularly effective. In other words, just ask them. Calling a customer who you know (or believe) had a great experience working with you is a great way to learn more about what you did well. You might ask questions as simple as;

"What was the best part of your experience in working with us?", and "what was the worst part of your service experience, or what do you think we can improve?" Often, the simple act of calling to inquire about their service experience improves their customer satisfaction, because calling proves you care.

By this point, you'll have an ideal customer avatar covering both demographics and psychographics. You will have a clear idea as to their goals, as well as their challenges (pain points). When you get to this level of customer intelligence, it's time to focus on you: specifically, your product or service, and its' features and benefits.

Step Three: Now it's your turn

Once you've spent this much time in your customer's shoes – you can finally craft your positioning statement. In order to do so, the third Post-it® exercise is to list off your skills, experience, and product and service features that are the perfect match to your customers' pain points, needs and goals. The goal here is not just to elevate your business in your customers' eyes, it is to differentiate. After all, as marketing expert and bestselling author Sally Hogshead put it in her book 'Fascinate', "different is better than better[11]".

When businesses and leaders go through the process in this order, the findings are quite profound. Instead of innovating your product or service in a vacuum, the light bulbs go off when companies realize exactly how they provide value to their customers (and when and if they don't). They might find simple 'low-hanging-fruit' fixes, or how a new innovation they were about to spend millions on might be a complete waste that adds little to no value in their customers' eyes.

Put simply, instead of going to market as "we make X, who needs that?", businesses can go to market as "we know this is who you are, and what you need/ struggle with, and so this is why we (make/sell) X.". As one of my mentors, Dr. Marilyn Taylor, professor of leadership studies at Royal Roads University puts it, "don't be an answer looking for a question".

Once you've completed your brainstorming, you can assign a priority sequence to your product and service features, and your company's competitive attributes. The elements that make up your value proposition should be ranked in a hierarchy, according to the effectiveness which they meet your customer's needs, and the urgency and importance of the problems they solve. In other words, the more value a product or service element adds in your customer's eyes, the more important that element becomes to your differentiation strategy.

As an example of ranking elements of one's value proposition, an accountant would likely miss a lot of opportunities if they positioned their practice with "providing timely and accurate financial statements". If they were also able to "provide insight into latent profit potential" for their customers, and didn't tell their prospects, they'd be missing out on a lot of their profit potential, too. Which of these solutions would you be more interested in as a business owner?

In the above example, the positioning statement at the heart of their value proposition says nothing of the accountants' experience, training, or credentials. Their value proposition speaks only to the value realized by their customers. If this was your accountant, would you really care what software they used, or where they went to school? As long as they help you stay tax-compliant in ethical ways, what you really care about is finding out where your business is leaving money on the table.

One other way many service professionals prefer to frame their value proposition is to take themselves out of the equation as much as possible. Consider the following two pitches from an investment advisor, and who would you choose?

Advisor One

"I went to an Ivy League school, graduated at the top of my class, became a CPA, and am a certified fiduciary. I've been an investment advisor for more than 15 years."

Advisor Two

"I've helped more than 300 families like yours reduce debt and achieve their financial goals over the last 15 years."

Who would you choose? When framing our value proposition, it's always important to remember who it should be about. Value is in the eye of the beholder, not the proprietor!

You (as a professional or as a company) become far more valuable when your focus is all about who you provide value to, and how you do it.

It's not about you

When we focus on the customer - and I mean *really* focus on the customer - we make it about them, not about us. It's important to maintain the focus on the customer, and on helping them at all times. We should never let our focus waver back to our own needs or problems. This is important for a couple of reasons.

First, our reality should not enter into the conversation. For instance, many luxury brands rely on young attractive people to sell their products and services. Imagine a 25 year-old selling multi-million-dollar condos in South Beach, Miami. The reality is most 25-year-olds might not be able to afford any of the apartments, condos or penthouse suites that they are showing. Imagine if this 25-year-old used words like 'expensive' or said things like "oh yeah, the monthly condo fees are really brutal here". This would clearly get in the way of most, if not all sales.

Now imagine if that same 25-year-old focused only on their ideal customer, and realized that this customer might have millions in the bank. They might even be a billionaire! If this young professional could keep their customers' reality in mind, they could start to make jokes like "the condo is only $500,000; the view is what you pay the extra million for". They can relate to their customer in ways that just aren't possible if they were too busy comparing bank accounts or the cars they drive.

I was running a fitness business in 2008 during the Global Financial crisis. Because our business was a discretionary spend for most people, it became very important for our team to get in front of as many customers as we could, as fast as we could, during a time where so many people were faced with such uncertainty.

I will never forget speaking to two of the customers I was most worried about losing. While I didn't know exactly what they made, I was pretty sure that these two made less than any of our other clients who were mostly highly successful executives and entrepreneurs.

Our strategy was to simply get in front of all of our customers to see how we can help them. We wanted to see if they needed to make any changes to their schedule, and how often they saw their trainer, in lieu of what was going on all over the world. These clients told me "don't worry about us. We will buy fewer groceries before we stop coming here". I have never forgotten that lesson, and how my values, and my budget, have nothing to do with my ideal client who's considering a purchase. It's about their priorities, not mine.

In 2017 I was meeting with a young professional who worked in energy. This client's goal was to climb the corporate ladder in the oil and gas sector. We went through our discovery session and hit it off pretty well. I then talked about the different packages and prices we have. I barely even mentioned our six-month package, because this person was several years younger than I was, and I somewhat expected that they were going to be asking me for a discount. Without hesitation, this client pulled out their credit card and paid for six months up front.

I had a story in my head about what this person could afford, or the value they placed on coaching. That story proved to be completely inaccurate, in fact it was downright wrong. This client was so driven to reach their goals, they paid for six months out of their own pocket up front. I've worked with senior executives who make more than $500,000 a year who only say yes to coaching if their organization pays for it. That moment reminded me to never insert my own values, goals or views on money into someone else's purchase decision. It's about them, it's not about me.

The second reason why we should not be focused on ourselves comes down to differentiation. It's hard, if not impossible, to stand out from our competition when we focus on our own needs. When we can become hyper-focused on the needs of our ideal customer, we can become an expert at solving their problems, and we might just be able to out-think our competition.

Not only can we build better products and improve our service offering by being highly attuned to the needs of our customer, but we can also help differentiate ourselves from our competitors by knowing what our customer needs better than anyone else.

Here are a few examples
- GoPro stands out among other cameras, not because their camera has more megapixels, but because they understand the lifestyle of their customers better than others. The camera can easily be mounted on different mounts; whether it's on handlebars, your bike helmet, your surfboard or the chest strap of your hydration backpack. GoPro makes it easy for their customers to look cool during their weekend warrior pursuits. It's also super easy to use a GoPro. It comes with a wrench to help change mounts. And what is on the back of that wrench? It's a bottle opener; because what do

weekend warriors do when they're finished their surfing session or shredding on their mountain bikes? They love to enjoy a cold one together. GoPro knows their audience.

- Speaking of a cold one, Coors Light knows that their audience enjoys their beer cold, so what did they do? "Don't drink it if those mountains aren't blue". Those are actual lyrics from the song "Pontoon" by Little Big Town. That's how iconic the temperature-activated blue mountains are on a can or bottle of Coors Light.

- Due to its massive size and relatively spread-out population, Canadian travelers know all too well the frustration and pain points associated with Canadian air travel. Relatively few competitors has led to high fares, especially when traveling to remote areas. Adding to Canadian's frustrations are the baggage fees, expensive Wi-Fi and expensive meals, snacks and drinks. For this reason, Porter Airlines, based out of Eastern Canada, has seen rapid growth in its customer base who love their free checked bags, free Wi-Fi, free food and even free spirits.

Dave Gerdhardt, Vice President of marketing at Drift, reminds us that, "customers have all the power in the buying process... as a result, whichever company makes it easier to buy is going to win. That's how we make decisions, today, as consumers[12]."

I can share a personal example of what happens when we don't take the time to understand our customers' needs or their reality. I've already mentioned that it's common for those in service-based industries to have a disconnect between providing the service, and being able to sell it confidently. Many professionals, like coaches, have limiting beliefs around sales and selling. For this reason, and because LinkedIn has made it easy to find any target market by location, company, and job title, coaches get pitched a lot. I mean a LOT.

On a typical week, I have to say no to between three and six salespeople offering me appointment-setting services, lead generation (lead gen), or high-ticket offer inbound lead services. Their due diligence on their target market of coaches has most likely informed them that a lack of leads, or predictable revenue, is one of the top pain points for all coaches. For this reason, they simply search 'coach' in the job title field of LinkedIn's search filters, and reach out to every coach they want to with their offer. As a coach who focuses on LinkedIn for my social media efforts, this makes me especially targetable.

Here's where these appointment-setters and lead magnets are missing the mark. They are all *pitching* me. Building a coaching business is hard. When the business is based on know, like, and trust, cold-calling doesn't work, Google Adwords and SEO optimization are expensive, and there are millions of coaches out there. If it's hard for me, and I've helped grow one of Canada's largest coaching practices, then it's hard for almost any coach. Is it possible there's an entire industry of sales rockstars out there who all have a database of executives and entrepreneurs wanting coaching who just can't find the right coach? No, it's not.

Almost every entrepreneur and executive knows at least one business, executive, or career coach, if not several. Most are just waiting to find the right one; one they can trust, who they feel has the right lived experience and background to help them achieve their goals and overcome their challenges. They might have already found the right one, but it might be the wrong timing in terms of cash flow, or their perceived ability to carve out an hour every week to meet with a coach.

The entire lead gen industry seems to rely on the 'sales is a numbers game' philosophy, rather than learning how to Never Sell Again by asking great questions, listening to understand, and then making a recommendation.

Full disclosure: I would have loved this service when I was starting my coaching journey, but no one got to know me, my reality, or how they could help. They were all too focused on what they were trying to sell.

The take home message here is this: stop trying to find a market to sell your product or service to. Find a market who has needs, goals, and challenges, and help them find what they are looking for. Sell what they are trying to buy, instead of trying to sell what you want to build. The best way to do this is to find a market segment that you truly care about. It might be accountants or lawyers, or it might be dentists or musicians. All that matters is that they matter to you, for whatever reasons you have.

Sometimes focusing on the customer means we make life inconvenient for ourselves, at least in the short term. It might be more convenient to meet a client over Zoom or Microsoft Teams than to get in your car and meet them at the coffee shop of their choice. It might be more convenient for you that your customer comes to your office, instead of you going to theirs all the time.

It might not be convenient for us, however when we consider what the customer wants at every point of their experience, we give them very few reasons to leave. We are building value every step of the way.

Marketing experts refer to the summation of a customer's experiences with a particular brand as the Customer Journey Map. When used as a strategic tool, the Customer Journey Map can help companies understand when and why they are providing excellent service experiences, and also when they are dropping the ball. It is at these moments that customers experience pain points with a particular brand. The greater the pain point and the more of them, the more likely that customer is to seek out an alternative solution. An example of a high-level Customer Journey Map used to generate procedures to maximize customer satisfaction is shown in Appendix B at the back of this book.

By adopting the Customer Journey Map as an ongoing strategy (this is a living document, not a one and done), sales professionals, entrepreneurs and organizations can become an invaluable partner for their customers who stay longer, spend more and refer more friends and family members. Don't try to set up a convenient lifestyle business if you really want to win. Try for impossible to beat. Watch what your customers do next!

The Never Sell Again approach is not just meant for salespeople. A great CEO is usually a great delegator. If they aren't, then that same CEO will find themselves as the bottleneck for their business. That being said, if the CEO and the entire team understand what is required of them, they stop defining their deliverables based on role or job title. This is especially important for senior leaders. Even if they've never worked a day in sales in their entire careers, many CEOs find themselves brought into sales conversations because of what's called 'role-to role selling'.

Regardless of how talented, experienced or even knowledgeable the sales team may be, some business owners only want to talk to the owner of the company they are considering doing business with. Sometimes the boss only wants to buy from the boss.

This is also true in different cultures. In some cultures, in different parts of the world, it might be considered rude for the owner of the company not to invest in the personal relationship with a potential strategic partner, vendor, customer or supplier. Some customers would be offended if they made their way to your corporate head office, only to find that the owner or CEO was too busy to meet them face to face. Delegation is important to run a smooth business, however it's not more important than the relationships each business is built upon. Don't assume what worked for you in Asia or America will work in Africa.

Less is more

You've probably heard the expression 'not all customers are created equally'. While this saying is true, there are layers to its' truth. Just like value is in the eye of the beholder (your customer), what makes a 'great' customer has a lot to do with the intersection of what they want, and what you offer.

We've talked about your ideal customer profile (ICP) making a purchase decision, but did you know they are actually making several decisions at once?

If you've been in sales (in any capacity) for longer than a week, you already know that price is one of the variables your ICP is weighing as they make a purchase decision. What else do you think they are grappling with?

The answer, as you may have guessed, is a lot of potential variables. As hard as that may be to play mind-reader for someone trying to help your ideal customer, I have good news. For most customers, we can put all of those potential variables into one convenient bucket.

In 2015 I took an Executive Education program in Sales Leadership at Queens University. There I had the great fortune of learning from Dr. Ken Wong. One of many nuggets I took from this program was Dr. Wong's take on customer segmentation.

Essentially, while your customer is deciding how much they want to pay for your product or service, they are also deciding which, of likely several options, is right for them. 'Right for them' comes down to fit, which comes down to alignment between product and service features, and their needs, priorities, and values.

Think of the last time you had to narrow down a search between several options. Perhaps you are considering purchasing a new barbeque. You might consider all of the following variables besides price:

1. Size
2. Color
3. How much heat the BBQ produces (measured in BTU)
4. Whether to go with a BBQ that uses charcoal, propane, or natural gas.
5. Brand
6. Whether or not it has that side heater to cook with a pan on your BBQ
7. Whether or not you can integrate your BBQ into your outdoor oasis (seamless integration with a brick and granite countertop and an outdoor fridge).

In this example, these seven variables make up the 'other decisions' your customer is making besides price. Essentially, without these seven variables, your customer will pick the lowest price every time. Based on which of these variables that matters the most to your ICP, they will weight their perceived product leaders against their price to determine their perceived value of your product or service.

Put simply, price is what we pay, value is what we feel it's worth.

I mentioned that we can place all variables besides price into one convenient bucket. According to Dr. Wong, this bucket can be named 'differentiation'. In other words, what sets your product or service apart from your competitors.

Essentially, your ideal customer is deciding how much they want to pay, and then measuring how important price is compared to differentiation. Last page you saw seven examples of differentiation for a product, namely a barbeque. Examples of differentiation for a service include:

1. Speed or timeliness (how fast you follow up, how quickly you can get in to see your massage therapist)
2. Quality or level of service (you simply do a better job than your competitors, whether it's answering their questions more fully, offering a better workout, or a more relaxing spa environment)
3. Better processes (a human answers the phone within three rings when you call, your service provider is always on time, you get timely follow up communication, as a few examples)
4. Qualifications (you might be the only person in North America certified to the level you are in your specific discipline)
5. Reputation (this is where five-star reviews, word of mouth, and experience help set a service provider apart – it's called 'social proof')
6. Fit – as subjective as it may be, the personality fit between a client and their coach, therapist, fitness trainer, or even doctor can't be taken for granted!

It was Theodore Roosevelt who coined the phrase "comparison is the thief of joy". Many consultants, coaches, or other service professionals tend to feel inferior when they go to a conference and hear the icons of their industry spew wisdom and confidence from the stage. It's true that not everyone can be John Maxwell, Brene Bown, or Tony Robbins, but you don't have to – while they're winning the reputation game, you have at least five other areas listed above that you can choose to compete or even win in your niche.

Getting back to the customer segmentation paradigm offered by Dr. Ken Wong at Queens University, your ICP is making two types of decisions at once; how much do they want to pay, and what do they want from their product or experience?

The intersection of these two decisions, price sensitivity, and importance placed upon differentiation, create a matrix containing four distinct customer quadrants.

Figure one on the following page demonstrates the intersection of price sensitivity and value on differentiation, and the four customer segments that the intersection of these decisions creates.

Figure One: Queens' Customer Segmentation Model

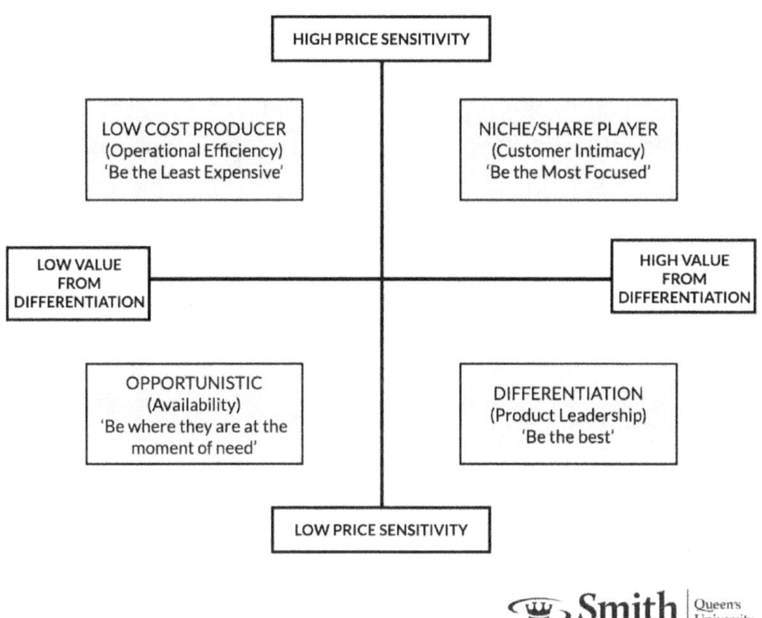

Essentially, the intersection of your ideal customer profile (ICP)'s values must become your differentiated strategy. You cannot be the lowest cost producer and the very best. Wine connoisseurs don't decide between $13 bottles of wine and $400 bottles, just like well-heeled travelers don't decide between a motel in an industrial area and the penthouse suite of a marquee hotel.

You can make money, and grow a great business, in any quadrant – unless you try to do so in all four. This is what business advisors mean when they say you have to 'choose your beachhead' – you need to make decisions about who you are – and who you are not – going to be as a business and as a brand.

Examples of each quadrant are below, so you know who you might want to emulate and why.

Low cost producer

Walmart. Why? Because they have mastered economies of scale. They have massive buying power, incredible distribution networks, and enviable market share. For these reasons, they can squeeze their suppliers (keep their costs very low), and still turn a profit, even with low prices. They make their money through modest margins and massive volume. The low cost producer thrives by selling to the price-conscious buyer.

Niche player

Paynter, based out of London, UK has niche down to an artform. They produce only four jackets a year (not a typo, just four). They are released made-to-order in limited release batches, At the time of publishing, according to their website, they had released just fifteen batches in their history and every jacket made has been sold. The niche player appeals to the value buyer, who focuses on value – what they are getting for what they pay.

Differentiation/ product leadership

You already know several brands that meet the 'gold standard'. Ferrari. Dom Perignon champagne. Harvard University. Four Seasons hotels. If these are your brands, you know you're going to pay more, but you gladly do so for the peace of mind that you are about to experience the very best, something no substitute can match. The product leader creates a relationship with their ideal buyer, even if it's one-way (buyers become a fan of the brand).

Opportunistic

Coca-Cola™'s go-to-market strategy can be summarized as 'be there at the moment of thirst'. Have you ever seen an ad for an ice cold Coke™ that was available at the convenience store on the corner of front street and fourth avenue? No. Coca-Cola™'s distribution is truly global. Their strategy is not awareness, or price, or highlighting product features. Every commercial is designed to imprint subliminal messages – emotions – with their product. Coke™ = fun with friends, being young and popular in summertime, and more. In doing so, people often grab a Coke™ not for 30 cents a can at Wal-Mart™, but for $2.50 at those little mini coolers near convenience store check-outs, or for $5.00+ at a music festival or the movies. Their strategy is to lead you towards an impulse purchase. The opportunistic seller tries to sell to the convenience buyer.

Now, most of us don't have Coca-Cola™'s advertising budget, and that's not the point either. The point is, using this segmentation model from Queens, is to apply the Never Sell Again philosophy. Get to understand your customer, their values, and their decision process so you are better prepared to serve them to the best of your abilities.

Rather than trying to be all things to all people, or force cookie cutter solutions across multiple customer segments, think about your ideal customer profile (ICP) and what matters to them. Now, consider your product or service, and how it offers them exactly what they want at the intersection of price and differentiation.

This helps you avoid getting dragged into every conversation being about price, and it helps your customer get what they are looking for at a price that is tolerable to them based on what they really want.

Once again, win-win scenarios underpin the Never Sell Again philosophy.

Speak their language

By this point you've come to understand your ideal customer profile (ICP)'s problems, pain points, goals, needs, and even values. You might be feeling more and more confident about the potential of your business, and/ or your career as you become more adept at serving your ICP and offering them more value.

As exciting as it is to learn new strategies, and feel more equipped to win in business, it's at this point I have to offer a cautionary reminder: not everyone speaks your language. I don't mean 'don't speak French in Japan'. I mean, people have different communicative styles. Your prospect might communicate differently than you are accustomed to communicating, and if you can't flex to their style, it's often harder for them to cross that 'know, like, trust' bridge.

Towards the end of my previous career (in health, fitness, and medical), our executive team brought in a skilled facilitator to help us gel as a leadership team after a recent merger. This facilitator was trained in a methodology called Core Strengths®. While we don't have room in this book to take a crash course in Core Strengths®, there are a few valuable lessons this methodology has to teach for any sales professional or entrepreneur.

First, people tend to act in accordance with their values and priorities[13]. This may not seem like rocket science, but there are important implications from this foundational principle. If people tend to act in accordance with their priorities and values, then it stands to reason that different people act or react differently, even to the same situation.

The Core Strengths® paradigm offers three distinct psychological profiles that are worth learning about in order to cater your approach to the communicative style of your prospect.

Red. The 'assertive-directing' type, 'red' types walk fast, talk fast, think fast, make decisions fast, and they are driven to win[13]. Red types are motivated by performance – they want to compete and earn their just rewards[13]. Often finding themselves in leadership positions, a red can justify forgiving their team for wasting money if it leads to learning, but most reds hate it when you waste their time[13].

Blue. Blue 'altruistic-nurturing' types are all about people[13]. Before they make a decision, they want to know how it affects the team, their customers, and their broader stakeholder base[13]. Blues can still be driven by performance, but the win they truly seek is a happy, harmonious team who loves what they do and where they do it[13].

Green. Green 'analytic-autonomizing' types are driven by order[13]. Greens love to swoop in behind visionary types, and add process, structure, efficiency, and even metrics and dashboards[13]. Greens aim for autonomy, efficiency, and predictability[13]. To make decisions, they need data and time – do not rush them[13]!

With this basic overview in mind, imagine this. You are a driven, borderline impatient red, demanding an immediate, and accurate, response from a green who needs time and data to give you what you need. It's a formula for conflict!

Now, imagine you and this green aren't teammates. Imagine you are a default red, and you are trying to sell to this green. Rushing them will just make them look elsewhere, and when they find a patient salesperson who gives them the information they need, and the time and patience to digest it, they will move their business to them.

Conversely, if you are a green, and you project your values onto a potential client who is a red, you will 'data them to death'. This red wants just enough info to make a decision, and they often expect it at the '50,000 square foot level', and you might be going deep down every rabbit hole on details they don't need or want to understand.

In either scenario, you aren't speaking their language. Now, most people haven't heard of Core Strengths®, so they're not going to tell you "I'm a blue – talk to me about how this affects my customers". Even so, you don't need to be a mind reader to speak their language.

By now you've heard the top two sales skills I've suggested over and over, so you know how to ask great questions and be a great listener. As is relates to speaking their language, listening will help you decode their native tongue. How? With the rate and tone of their speech, what questions they ask, and how they deal with time.

For example, if your prospect asks you questions about how your software integrates with their existing tech stack, and asks you to slow down (if you are glazing over the details), you're likely dealing with a green. Give them time and data!

If your prospect prefers to meet you at a coffee shop in person rather than their office or over Zoom, they might be a blue. In this case, the relationship is a big part of the sales process and decision, it's not just the X's and O's of your product or service features.

And finally, if all roads lead back to ROI (return on investment), and you detect a baseline sense of speed or urgency to everything they do, you're likely selling to a red. Get to the point. Sell the outcome, not the process. Thank them for their time and end the meeting on time, if not early.

Speaking their language is a sign of respect, if not care. If you want to avoid being commoditized, and the 'race to the bottom' that comes with becoming a commodity, take the time to get to know who you are dealing with, and show them the respect of speaking their language.

It sounds simple, but it never ceases to amaze me how many entrepreneurs and sales professionals skip this step. Remember, your prospect is one in eight billion – they are not a 'walking commission'!

Caring is a great strategy

Earlier in this book, I mentioned that the Never Sell Again approach is something that you can't fake. The reason it can't be faked is because you can't fake caring. People can tell when you care, and they can tell when you are just 'checking a box'. This next strategy should only ever be used if you truly care about your customers.

As part of the complete Customer Journey Map, and as part of a comprehensive service process, we encourage a three-step customer service check-in for all current and dormant customers with whom you've not spoken in a while (two – six months depending on the nature of your business).

This three-step check-in process helped one landscaper I coached several years ago secure more than $75,000 in new projects through less than 10 phone calls, without him ever having to 'sell'.

The 3-step check-in process is below:

1. Service Check-in (phone call)

"Hi Cory, I just wanted to check in, as you are one of [my/our] best customers, and I wanted to see how your [product or service] has been treating you. Any issues or concerns?"

If yes – fix the problem and end the call with "is there anything else I can help you with?"

If no – "that's great, I'm glad our [product or service] is working for you! If you don't mind my asking, how satisfied would you say you are with your overall service experience with us on a scale of 1-10?" (one being terrible, 10 being amazing)

If they score you between one and eight, ask what went wrong (if low) or what prevented their experience from being a nine or a ten. Thank them for their feedback, even if it hurts to hear.
If they score you a nine or a ten – proceed below to step two and three.

Remember the top two sales skills – asking profound questions and then listening with your whole body. During the call (if they're happy) listen for cross-sell or up-sell opportunities ("that's great that [insert what they just told you] – did you know we also sell [insert recommendation]?")

2. Testimonial ask

If they gave a complimentary answer during step one, simply ask, "I'm so glad to hear your experience was that positive [insert name]. Would you mind if I captured your sentiments in the form of a testimonial for our website and other marketing efforts? You can be mentioned by company and/ or name, your initials, or be left completely anonymous. I can send you what I wrote down for your approval or any edits first if that helps."

This makes it easy for them, and you get to control the quality of the testimonial!

3. Referral ask

Building off of the testimonial from above step: "I/we've certainly enjoyed working with you as well [insert customer name]. In fact, we'd love to work with more customers just like you. Who can you think of in your network who would enjoy working with us as much as you have?" or "who else in your network needs our service?"

In the above example, it's important to ask 'who do you know?', not 'do you know anyone?' Asking your client who they know leads them to think about names. Asking if they know anyone who needs your service right now is a yes or no answer, and most days – it's a no. Remember: *ask great questions* and listen with your whole body.

My good friend, expert connector and recruiter, and co-author of How to Sell in Any Economy, Catherine Brownlee, advises her clients that every person in your network who truly wants to help you will, over time, be good for up to four or five potential referrals. This means the three-step check-in process is something you can use over and over again every year or two with every customer. Even for a small business this can be completely transformative.

A full-time coach, for example usually works less than 10 to 15 hours a week actually coaching paying clients. Even if they have 10 clients and use the three-step check-in process over a few years, that's potentially 50 referrals. That's enough clients to potentially last one coach a career, or enough opportunity to build a team and scale a company. Don't forget Catherine's other great advice with this approach – we must always follow up with those who send us referrals and thank them!

One important caveat to leveraging your network and the referrals it could bring is to never pull the 'bait and switch'. In other words, don't build the relationship as the face of the company (especially in a service-based business), and then pawn your new customer off on your most junior service provider. Your relationship capital doesn't transfer to your junior team member after you 'close the deal'. This doesn't mean you need to be the full-time business development person and the only service provider. It does mean that you must be candid and transparent about your role, and what your new customer can expect in doing business with you.

As the business development lead or business owner, you can introduce new customers to the business and maintain a relationship with them by checking in from time to time to ask how the service is going. You might act as a concierge of their service experience post-sale. Maintaining this type of relationship also helps to retain customers, as team members inevitably change jobs or careers. Some will even spin off their own copycat business and try to steal your customers. It happens in every industry, and you can never fully prevent it. Even so, keeping tabs on how your customers' service experience is going does go a long way in keeping them as customers after their service delivery lead exits your company.

Never Sell Again isn't just about sales

The concept of Never Selling Again applies to many more aspects of business and daily life than just sales. Remember Dan Pink's survey. 40% of our time is spent in sales-like situations[2]. If we spend 40% of our days negotiating, bartering or trying to influence others, then we must apply the Never Sell Again principles to almost anything that we do. Here are just a few examples of how to Never Sell Again, yet get better results in various areas of life:

- Networking. Rather than telling people what you do or asking them for a job, or trying to sell to them, remember the two most important sales skills. Ask great questions, and listen with your whole body. People love to answer questions about themselves and their business. (hint: if your business is in the B2B sector, asking questions about other people's business helps you position yours. This is the heart of level four selling according to John Hoskins[3]). In fact, I wrote this section of the book in July of 2023. In the last month I've attended five networking events and one conference. Networking with a Never Sell Again mentality has led to six meetings this week with professionals I've met at these networking events. I had three meetings left to go in the week at the time of writing, and I'd already received a referral for a new client from one of these meetings. I also had two more requests for meetings, and booked another for next week. This was in a week that I was only working three days, because my son and I were going camping the rest of the week. Most of our clients come by way of referrals and networking, which means I truly never have to 'sell'.

- Job interviews. If you find yourself looking for work and happen to be in an interview situation, apply the Never Sell Again philosophy. Of course, you need to promote your experiences and your skills, but it becomes much easier to do so when you find out more about the company you hope to work for. Do your homework in advance. Learn about the company's history, organizational values and philosophies, as well as their key customers and growth plans. Depending on the size or nature of the business, most of this information can easily be found in the press section of their website. Publicly traded companies will have their report to shareholders information available on their website. In addition to your due diligence before the interview, asking great questions will help you position yourself better. You might ask questions about the organizational culture. You might ask about the company's growth plans, or who their main competitor is. You might ask questions about the biggest obstacles the organization foresees to its growth strategies. In any case, asking great questions helps you position yourself as their ideal candidate. Some people like to ask why the position is available. Take caution that this question could be seen as accusational. An interviewer may feel that you are making an accusation about the work culture or the work environment by insinuating that this position would not be open, had the last person not quit.
- Saving money. It never hurts to ask for a discount when making a purchase. It's true that you don't get

what you don't ask for. However, think to yourself: 'what's in it for the other person to give you a discount?' On the surface, the only thing that's in it for them is a smaller commission or profit. It's not in their best interest to give you a discount. If you want to avoid paying full retail prices, your job is to make it in their best interest to give you a discount. How can you do this? By applying the Never Sell Again philosophy. Ask them questions. Get to know them, and their business. Perhaps you've got a large network. Help them understand that giving you a discount might bring them more customers. You might tag them on social media, specifically the salesperson you dealt with, and the location you visited. You might not talk about the discount, but you might talk about the quality of the product or service, and what an amazing experience you had. By giving them exposure, perhaps the salesperson feels they can reciprocate by giving you a discount. Now you're not just asking them to make less money, you are offering value, which they may in return reciprocate as a discount for you.

- Asking for a favor. We all need help from time to time. Whether we are moving, trying to lift a heavy couch or landscaping our backyard, we all need help from our friends, family or neighbors now and then. Asking for a favor is just another example of where the Never Sell Again philosophy can work wonders. Rather than just asking for a favor and not reciprocating, you might lead with an offer, even though an ask is on its way. The typical reward for helping a friend move is beer and pizza. How much more likely to find help would you be if you used a barter system instead? Perhaps you are a resume writer and you need help moving. Would your friends rather a few slices of pizza and a pop or beer, or having you review and improve their resume for free in exchange for their help? Perhaps the friend you asked for help runs a small business. Instead of pizza, they might prefer that you give their business a five-star review on Google, or shout out their small business on your social media platforms. Maybe you just buy something from their store the next time you have a need that they happen to sell. There are lots of ways of helping our friends who help us.

- Asking for a raise. The truth is, life is expensive, and most people have trouble keeping up to the pace of inflation. Even with cost-of-living adjustments, many employees find themselves falling behind, rather than keeping up. That being said, don't ask for a raise the way some employees have asked me, citing that their rent went up and so they need a raise. For many jobs, the wage is set as a percentage of the revenue collected for providing a service, or selling a projected number of products. For instance, a massage therapist who wants to be paid more needs to remember that their employer needs to pay the lease for the building, marketing and advertising costs to attract customers, as well as things like massage tables, sheets, and massage oils. This doesn't necessarily mean that they don't deserve a raise. Keep in mind that increasing your income can take on many forms. This massage therapist might offer to work more hours, in addition to asking for a raise. They might also offer their clients the massage oils or essential oils used during the treatments for sale. This all helps bring in more revenue, which can help offset the increased labor wage they are asking for. The point is, just as in every other scenario, put yourself in your employers' shoes. Having a tough time making ends meet is a problem, but your employer is far more likely to work with you when you lead with solutions, rather than trying to pass your problems onto them. Whatever your position, company, industry, or city you work in - try asking your employer questions about the problems they are trying to solve. By trying to be part of the solution, your employer is more likely to view you as an asset to the company, rather than a liability. By trying to add more value to your employer and to your company, you are more likely to receive greater value in return.

You might even apply the Never Sell Again philosophy to asking your spouse to make time for a date night. In short, we get more of what we want by helping others get what they want and need. Rather than focusing on what you need, lead by asking yourself, 'what's in it for them?' WIIFT (what's in it for them) is the key to Never Selling Again. And if you don't know WIIFT – *ask!*

Old School solutions for the new world

We live in a fast-paced, ever-changing world. With the advent of artificial intelligence (AI) tools like ChatGPT, or machine learning and robotic process automation, many professionals worry that their skill set is at risk of becoming obsolete. In fact, thousands have already lost their jobs to robots or lower cost outsourced solutions. In any business, one must ask themselves how to remain relevant if they hope to remain successful.

With the advances being made in artificial intelligence, the soft skills and emotional intelligence required to create authentic and meaningful relationships are more important than ever. If you want to future-proof your resume, get better at asking amazing questions and listening with your whole body. If you want to matter to your customers and to your business, learn how to move from transactional sales to serving your customers through their entire journey with your organization.

A human can't compete with a machine when it comes to productivity or physical work capacity. No matter how complex the machine, or its operating software or algorithms, no machine is a match for human creativity, compassion or connection. The domain of sophisticated sales, leadership, and relationships are great places to focus one's career should you hope to find yourself 'future-proof'.

There's an old saying that your paycheck is proportional to the size of the problems you solve. Perhaps you're not solving the largest problems that your customer segment has. This doesn't mean you can't enjoy a remarkably rewarding and fulfilling career. By shifting your focus from the transaction to helping, you earn more opportunities to help your customer with more problems. In business terms this leads to higher customer retention, higher customer lifetime value (CLV) and more referrals. In plain English, more revenue for your business and more money for you. It's the great irony of the Never Sell Again philosophy: you and your company reap more profit when you focus on your customer, not just your profit margin.

Don't forget, it does take work. There are no shortcuts. No approach, strategy or system works if you don't. As you consider the suggestions and strategies in this book, consider one more peculiar paradox. We often tend to sell differently than we buy.

Think about making a major purchase. It doesn't have to be a home or a car, just something significant. Imagine the process of buying a new major appliance like a fridge. Chances are, you've done your homework, and you know the dimensions that would fit your kitchen. You are probably replacing an old fridge, in which case you're looking for something nicer and newer. You might also be purchasing a new refrigerator as part of a kitchen renovation, in which case you might be going with all stainless steel appliances, or a certain color scheme.

Research has shown, in fact, that by the time the seller even meets their prospective buyer, that buyer is already 57% of the way or more through the buying process[4]. All a prospective buyer needs or wants at this point, is to have their last few questions answered, or as one of my clients put it, 'to intellectually justify their emotional purchase'.

Based on how they want to buy, the ideal salesperson would only need to greet this more-than-halfway-done-buyer, ask them a few questions like what brought them in today, and then make a recommendation after hearing their customer out.

It's a convenient win-win: the customer does not want to be hassled. The salesperson, in doing less hassling, doesn't have to work as hard. The customer wants a resource, not a recurring pest. They want a problem-solver, not a pushy salesperson.

Now, let's consider how we often sell. From awkward cold-calls, to one-size fits all pitches, we tell ourselves that 'sales is a numbers game', and we feel like a failure if we're not the world's best copywriter, or most gregarious extrovert. In other words, instead of meeting one prospect at a time where they're at with their purchase and in their life, we try to push a macro-approach on a specific subset of the population at large. You might as well call every potential customer by the same name. Buyers don't want cookie-cutter, they want custom.

Why don't we just sell the way we want to buy? It sounds like common sense, doesn't it? While there are, of course, marked differences from one buyer's expectations to the next, this is for the most part just that - common sense. Just be the help that your customer is looking for, and you will never be out of work, and you will never have to work that hard for a sale.

Never Sell Again.

Instead, show up as the best version of yourself, poised, prepared, and ready to help.

It's how people want to buy, and it's how they'll buy more from you.

Pages Into Points: The Never Sell Again System

The Never Sell Again System can be summarized into the following 16 strategies and philosophies:

1. Find a market subset that you truly care about
2. Complete your Ideal Customer Profile (ICP) described on pages 45 – 48.
3. Define your value proposition, as described on pages 49 – 52.
4. Grow your network of your ICP's. Attend networking events, ask for referrals, join relevant industry associations. Fish where the fish are.
5. When you meet with your ideal potential customer, make the focus on them, not you.
6. Get to know your potential customer by asking great questions, and listening with your whole body
7. Always remember that what we used to consider selling, when it is done at the highest level, is actually just customer service that happens 'pre-contract'.
8. When you have asked, listened, and heard your prospects' pain points, needs, and goals, it's your job to provide them a solution, not a sale. It becomes your moral obligation to serve your customer to the best of your ability.
9. Offer what they need. Remember the Queens' segmental model. Those looking to buy a Ferrari aren't asking about fuel efficiency, and opportunistic buyers aren't likely to drive across town just for a deal.
10. Add more value than anyone else. Create a Customer Journey Map to identify all of the key

interactions your customer has with you, and find ways to wow them at every turn.

11. Check in from time to time, not to sell but to serve. Not for the commission, but because you care. Make the three-step check in process on pages 73 – 76 a part of your routine business strategy.
12. Speak their language. Don't rush a 'green' or waste a 'red's' time.
13. Never let a customer wonder whether you care about them or not. Be proactive, and be intentional.
14. In other areas of life, from favors to fundraising, keep the focus on others' needs, and find a way to serve them. The chances of you getting what you need multiply.
15. Sell like you want to buy, not like you need the sale. Put yourself in your customers' shoes.
16. Go tell others. Give them a copy of this book, or lend them yours. Business must be a force for good. What a world we would live in if all businesses made the world a better place in at least some way, shape or form!

Appendix A

The 3 Step Never Sell Again Process

Goal

To reverse engineer your biggest raving fans, in order to more easily find more of them.

Process

If you're a new business – go as deep as you can with who you think will be your ideal customer. If you're an established business, perform a spend analysis, or go through the below exercise with your 'best customers' in mind. Platforms like Quickbooks or your point-of-sale (POS) software can easily organize your customers by lifetime or annual spend, from highest to lowest. This gives real data on who your best customers are, rather than guessing.

Outcome

While the process will likely be very detailed, and also time-consuming in the beginning, the outcome objective is to arrive at a clear statement that will give your team, and biggest supporters, a concise idea of exactly who would be a great candidate to refer to your business.

FSQ Consulting's executive leader customer avatar statement is below as an example:

"Amir has spent 20+ years in various finance roles climbing the corporate ladder. He has been building his financial skills and financial modeling capabilities ever since he started at his first junior energy company. Decades later, he is now the Senior Vice President of Finance at A1 Corporation. Amir reports directly to the CFO, and is shocked to see that despite being a senior executive at a publicly traded company, his boss's leadership skills leave much to be desired. Amir needs to learn better communication strategies. He wants to know how to 'manage above', as well as work with some of his senior peers, who seem right at home in a 'dog eat dog world'. Amir is wondering if he should explore his career options elsewhere, but there is so much about A1 he loves, and a significant financial risk to moving on elsewhere. Amir needs someone as versed in leadership, coaching, and team effectiveness as he is in finance."

Step 1: Your Ideal Customer

Demographics (B2C)

Age (range)
Profession
Career/ Life stage
Annual income
Where do they live?
Family situation
Important lifestyle info
Other factors

Demographics (B2B)

Years in business
Industry
Company size
Annual revenue

Location(s)
Other factors

Psychographics

What are their pain points?

-
-
-
-
-

What problems are they trying to solve?

-
-
-
-
-

What are their goals?

-
-
-
-
-

How do they make their purchase decisions?

1. How do they select potential vendors?
2. How do they shortlist vendors?
3. How do they do their research (i.e. friends, Google, online reviews)?

What are their Core Values?

-
-
-
-

What are brands they identify with?

-
-
-
-

What key 'trigger events' or circumstances lead them to cross the 'purchase threshold' and make a purchase? (examples – a loved one has a health scare so you buy life insurance, or you miss out on a promotion so you go back to school, or a lower cost provider doesn't show up on install day so you up your budget and go with the more expensive but more trustworthy company)

Statement:

("Sarah is…" or "ABC company is…")

Step 2: Your Unique Value Proposition

Based on the above context, why are you valuable to your ideal customer or client? Why are you different or special? How do your skills, experience, and wisdom solve their problems and pain points, and help them achieve their goals – to a degree, and within a time frame that is worth paying for?

Brainstorm:

-
-
-
-
-
-
-

Trends:

-
-
-
-

Statement:

-

Step 3: Your Irresistible Offer

Now that you know why you are valuable (or more valuable or different) to your ideal customer; your first reaction is probably to go headfirst into prospecting mode. It makes sense, because now you can more succinctly frame why your product or service is compelling to them. While your motivation to meet with them might be clear and obvious, why should they meet with you? How can you convey the notion of meeting with you as being urgent and in their best interest in an email or phone call?

This is why we need a 'hook'- an offer that gets them to take notice, have a desire, maybe even a little bit of F.O.M.O. (fear of missing out) – and take the meeting.

Past examples:

1. FSQ Consulting's value proposition is getting driven, values-based leaders unstuck and making progress towards their goals and dreams. The service we provide is coaching and consulting, made specifically valuable to this audience by our proprietary R.E.S.U.L.T.S. process that is based on measuring – and providing – ROI in the form of i) financial, ii) measured improvements in business acumen, and iii) compressed success timelines. We often achieve all three, but as compelling as that may be, we get the meeting by offering a free, no-obligation coaching discovery session. Our prospects can test what they get before they commit, and we promise to teach them something new about their business, or solve one of their problems for free within the hour. In that first meeting, I usually give a free copy of one of my bestsellers – How to Sell in Any Economy or Success is a System, depending on the specific goals of the proposed coaching engagement. Free bestseller & free coaching session from the author conveys at least $550 in value for an hour of a prospects time - $555 if you include the coffee!

2. Toronto search group (not their real name). We worked with a recruitment firm whose sales were really suffering. They went through steps one and two above, which lead them to change their website to better convey their value proposition, not just their services. Their irresistible offer (remember-recruitment firm) was a free succession-planning tool we created. There were formulas built into a protected MS Excel document that accounted for all

of the variables our client could identify that might lead to a key team member leaving or retiring. Their clients could use this tool as part of their annual strategic planning. At a time when their clients were struggling, our client was able to land more meetings in two months than they had in the previous year to demonstrate the succession-planning tool. Not to mention, during the meeting they got to ask if there were any immediate needs, and every year when their clients used the tool – the recruiters contact information was one click away in the tool itself!

3. State of the industry report. We helped another client in the leadership space with their irresistible offer. They were a new company, with a relatively small network, who were having a hard time getting the meeting with the right decision makers. We decided to use that challenge as a strategy. Because decision makers were hard to reach – instead of a direct sales strategy, we created a list of questions that spoke directly to their clients' pain points. They then aggregated the answers from several decision makers to create a hyper-localized 'state of the industry report'. From there, they had a second touch point. They were able to follow up with their prospects to go through the state of the industry report they'd created. In that meeting, the trends were highlighted, including their competitor's answers to "what have you tried to solve xyz problems?" The best part? Their business really was the solution to these problems, so this strategy was like shining a flashlight on the clients' best solution right in front of their eyes.

Crafting Your Offer

As you craft your offer, there are a few important tips to keep in mind;

1. Never lose sight of the end goal: solve your customers pain through your core product or service. You can't solve a problem you don't know about, so you need to remember to ask great questions and listen with your whole body.
2. Value beats price almost every time. Your offer doesn't have to be a discount. Value usually has to be seen, and better yet experienced, to be perceived. In your lead nurturing process, find ways to give your prospect value before you charge them anything.
3. Sometimes a taste is all anyone needs. How many times do you buy the cinnamon bun or the fresh baked pretzel if the mall kiosk gives you a free sample? Find ways of delivering a portion of your value proposition – and that can be your hook or irresistible offer. You might be able to sell your course through a free webinar or book, etc.
4. Find ways to assign value. The more you can drive up the perceived and real value of your offer, the better (and more irresistible) your offer becomes. A free coaching or strategy session with an author for instance, delivers usually a 20x- 100x multiple on the value of the book itself. Rent out a mountain cottage and partner with a catering company, and now you have a weekend experience. Add a hike, snowshoe, or dog sled, plus a full day of strategic facilitation with you, and now your time and some pre-planning is a $5,000 - $25,000 experience. If you run a consulting company that charges six or seven figures a year for

enterprise-level solutions, this is a great way to build personal relationships with the right decision makers as you get them already started on their process ("why would we start over with someone new when we already spent the whole weekend doing this with ABC Consulting?")

Your Offer Ideas

-
-
-
-
-
-

Appendix B

Customer Journey Map Example – *financial advisory firm*

	Customer expectation	Company deliverable
Inquiry	Person, not machine answering phone Should be able to find you on Google Want to see lots of positive reviews Helpful FAQs on website Directions on website Parking easy to find	Answer phone within 3 rings Top 10 FAQs written up as blog post on website Update contact us page Move parking sign so it can be seen from the street
Intake	Receptionist should acknowledge me when I walk in Company representative should be friendly and professional Meeting should take less than 30 minutes Forms shouldn't be too long	Eye contact upon entry Standardized script with a smile every time a customer walks in All team members wearing company uniform Develop an 'intake meeting flow' to keep it tight and consistent for all team members Review and shorten intake form
Onboarding	Welcome email sent within 12	Welcome email template created

	hours of intake meeting, should come from the person I met with (or their boss or company owner). Transferring my investments over should not be painful.	Welcome emails from day all go out end of day. Step by step guide to transferring their investments written as article and link to article included in welcome email.
Service delivery	Advisor should meet with me at set intervals (my choice whether quarterly, twice a year, or annually). Advisor should email me from time to time to check in I want a detailed performance summary monthly. Advisor should call me when major local or global economic events occur.	Set meeting frequency with client, place in client and advisor's calendar and into internal system. Monthly performance summaries sent. All advisors must do a 'random check in' with their clients every quarter unless specified otherwise by client. All clients are called when major events that could affect their investments occur.
Misc.	It should be easy to withdraw all or some of my investments. I expect my advisor to act in my best interests, not what makes them the most commission.	Analyze and expedite the withdrawal process. All advisors are fiduciaries, not commission-based. Hand written card and a dinner gift

	I should be thanked for sending this company referrals. I prefer (to be/ not to be) emailed on my birthday or anniversary of joining the firm.	certificate sent for all referrals. Email all clients on birthdays and anniversary of joining (except those who opt out).

References

1. Mehrabian, Albert. <u>Silent Messages</u> 1971. Wadsworth publishing
2. Pink, Dan. <u>To Sell is Human</u> 2013. Riverhead books
3. Hoskins, John. <u>Level 5 Selling</u> 2016. Amazon publishing
4. https://www.propellercrm.com/blog/sales-statistics
5. https://www.forbes.com/sites/forbesagencycouncil/2017/08/25/finding-brand-success-in-the-digital-world/?sh=5bbed395626e
6. https://www.forbes.com/sites/bradjaphe/2023/06/12/dwayne-johnson-talks-about-launching-the-fastest-growing-tequila-of-all-time/?sh=1bc94ada4281
7. https://images.forbes.com/forbesinsights/StudyPDFs/Business_Meetings_FaceToFace.pdf
8. Oosterveld, Ben. <u>The Richest Real Estate Agent</u>. 2022. Lioncrest publishing
9. https://explodingtopics.com/blog/startup-failure-stats
10. https://www.business2community.com/marketing/your-value-proposition-is-not-about-you-02385577
11. Hogshead, Sally. <u>Fascinate: How to make your brand impossible to resist</u> 2016. Harper Business
12. Sheridan, Marcus. <u>They Ask, You Answer: A Revolutionary Approach to Inbound Sales, Content Marketing, and Today's Digital Consumer</u> 2017. Wiley
13. Scudder, Tim. <u>Working With SDI 2.0</u>. Core Strengths Inc. 2021

Acknowledgements

Nothing great happens without a team, and every project, every business, and every book I've ever been a part of has been a team effort.

The team I'd like to thank this time around includes Taryn Lipschitz for the brilliant cover design, and being patient with me through every redesign!

Thank you to Marie-Claude (MC) Lessard and Layla Binesh for catching a few grammatical or spelling errors that slipped past my normally obsessive edits.

Thank you to John Hoskins, Catherine Brownlee, Diana Pederson, Michael Palmer, Dave Barwise, Miguel Abascal, Erik Greenstein and Layla Binesh for taking the time to read Never Sell Again in advance, and for your kind praise. Your expertise is valuable, your opinion respected, and your time appreciated!

Thank you to the team at FSQ Consulting, and to all of our clients, who grant me the opportunity every day to do what I love, serve others, constantly learn, and get better as a person and professional while finding new ways to serve others.

Lastly, thank you as always to my family and friends who support me in all my endeavors, and bear with me as the demands of doing what I love take me away from who I love. You are why I do what I do, you are who I want to celebrate the wins with, and you are who I turn to when the wins aren't happening as fast or as often as I would hope. You could roll your eyes less, and laugh at my dad jokes more, but the support is appreciated nonetheless!

About the author

Stan Peake has spent the last 25 years helping thousands of leaders discover and live up to their potential. With entrepreneurial experience spanning eight businesses, Stan has started, bought into, closed, and sold businesses. As an executive, Stan has been a part of five leadership teams in the last quarter century. He has hired, developed, and helped shape the careers of over 400 professionals in his career.

Stan holds a graduate certificate in values-based leadership from Royal Roads University, an executive education in Sales Leadership from Queens University, and a certificate in Entrepreneurship and Innovation from Harvard Business School Online. Stan is certified as an executive coach, a corporate facilitator, and as a practitioner of cultural transformation tools.

In his role as Co-Founder and Director of Leadership Development, Stan oversees the coaching and leadership development services for FSQ Consulting Inc, including a team of over 35 executive coaches in five countries. When not coaching others or leading FSQ's team of expert coaches, Stan is a regular speaker at business and leadership conferences. He has also written for several magazines and publications, including Entrepreneur, Bizztor Media (India's largest publication for entrepreneurs), and Choice Magazine, the industry magazine for coaches. US Insider listed Stan as one of the top 10 executive coaches to follow in 2023, alongside Tony Robbins and Jay Abraham. Stan's 2021 TEDx talk, "Lasting Happiness is an Inside Job" has been viewed over 110,000 times on YouTube.

Never Sell Again is Stan's 8th book. Five of his previous titles became bestsellers on Amazon, including the #1 bestsellers *How to Sell in Any Economy* and *Now What? 50 ways to build your business in a crisis*. Stan is also a business advisor and investor, with a diverse portfolio of entrepreneurs and businesses he has been supporting since 2016.

Giving back is also very important to Stan and his family. Stan volunteers his time to speak at universities each year about leadership and entrepreneurship. Stan has been organizing a neighborhood cleanup each Earth Day since 2018. Peake is a regular contributor to the National Coalition Against Domestic Violence, as well as Operation Underground Railroad, which frees children from modern day slavery and trafficking. Stan is on a mission to raise, donate, and organize donations of over $10 million dollars for worthy causes in his lifetime. Stan has also served on several volunteer boards, from children's organizations to local community organizations.

Stan resides in Calgary, AB, Canada with his wife Maria, son Chase, and dog Zeke.

To reach Stan:
Stan@getsuccessfaster.com
www.getsuccessfaster.com
https://www.linkedin.com/in/stanpeake/